Dear Parent:

Your child's love of reading starts here!

Every child learns to read in a different way and at his or her own speed. Some go back and forth between reading levels and read favorite books again and again. Others read through each level in order. You can help your young reader improve and become more confident by encouraging his or her own interests and abilities. From books your child reads with you to the first books he or she reads alone, there are I Can Read Books for every stage of reading:

SHARED READING
Basic language, word repetition, and whimsical illustrations, ideal for sharing with your emergent reader

BEGINNING READING
Short sentences, familiar words, and simple concepts for children eager to read on their own

READING WITH HELP
Engaging stories, longer sentences, and language play for developing readers

READING ALONE
Complex plots, challenging vocabulary, and high-interest topics for the independent reader

I Can Read Books have introduced children to the joy of reading since 1957. Featuring award-winning authors and illustrators and a fabulous cast of beloved characters, I Can Read Books set the standard for beginning readers.

A lifetime of discovery begins with the magical words "I Can Read!"

Visit www.icanread.com for information
on enriching your child's reading experience.

The Cool Bean Makes a Splash
Text copyright © 2024 by Jory John
Illustrations copyright © 2024 by Pete Oswald
Interior illustrations by Saba Joshaghani in the style of Pete Oswald

Library of Congress Control Number: 2023943324
ISBN 978-0-06-332956-0 (trade bdg.)—ISBN 978-0-06-332954-6 (pbk.)

24 25 26 27 28 LBC 5 4 3 2 1   First Edition

READING 2 WITH HELP

I Can Read!

THE COOL BEAN
MAKES A SPLASH

Written by Jory John

Cover illustration by Pete Oswald

Interior illustrations by Saba Joshaghani based on artwork by Pete Oswald

HARPER

An Imprint of HarperCollinsPublishers

4

WATCH OUT!

Here come the cool beans.

Check out how
they dive!

Look at how they
cannonball!

Watch how they
backflip!
YOW!

6

What a splashy entrance.
The cool beans are the best
swimmers in town.

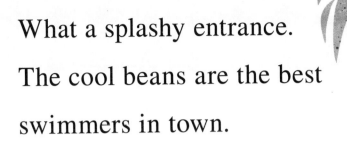

"Ahhhhhh, yes.
This is the life."

Look at their terrific technique.

Their perfect posture.

Their fearless floating.

The cool beans are at
the center of everything.

Meanwhile, I'm out here on my own.

I'm treading water by myself.

But hey, we're all just doing our best.

Plus, there are plenty of things

for an ordinary bean to do in the pool.

I can still have a grand ol' time.

Yes.

But every time I try to act cool . . .

. . . it never goes very well.

Hmm.

Hmmmmmm.

Suddenly I have a NEW idea.

A BIG idea. A SUPER idea.

Have you seen the super slide?

Up there?

See? Wayyyyyy up there?

You see it?

Yes, it's huge.

Yep, it's tall.

Yeah, it's scary.

12

13

I've never been brave enough
to ride on the slide before.
Maybe today's my day.

After all, how will I ever
become a cool bean
if I don't take a chance?

So now I have a plan. Yes.

I'm going to gracefully glide

down the super slide!

WATCH OUT!

Here I come, marching up the steps.

WATCH OUT!

Here I am, about to ride the super slide

to fame and glory.

WATCH OUT!

Here . . . I . . . um . . . here . . . uh . . .

Um . . . why are my knees shaking?

And why do my arms feel like noodles?

And why am I sweating?

And why am I wobbly?

And why is my stomach

filled with butterflies?

"Gulp."

Oh no. No no no.

Look. Down there. See?

Everybody's staring at me!

I can't do it.

I just can't do it.

I don't know what I was thinking.

Oh no, what are the cool beans doing?

Wait . . . why are they coming up here?

Wait . . . are they going to embarrass me even more?!

I can't stand it.

ARRRGGGHHH!

It turns out, the cool beans

just wanted to help me out.

Oh, and they asked if I'd like
to ride the slide WITH them.
They're waiting for my answer.

"Um . . . well . . .
uh . . . I mean . . . sure . . . yes . . .
I would like that."

24

25

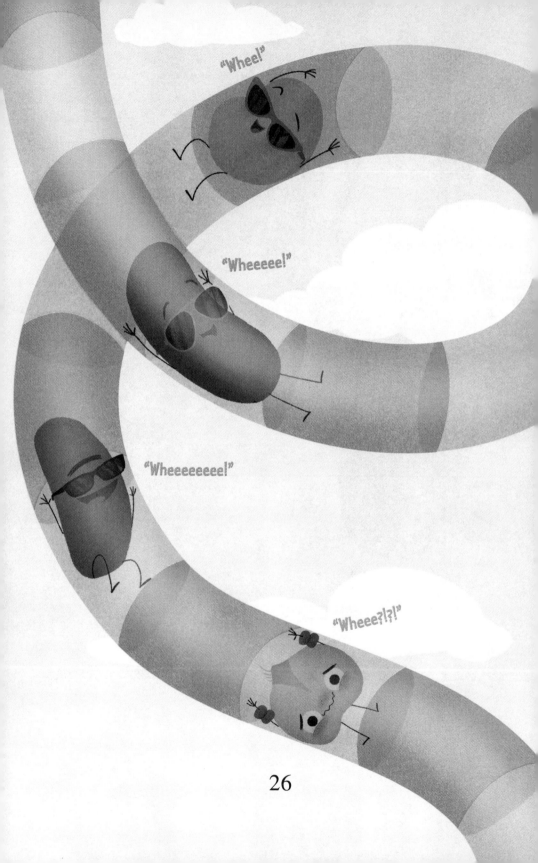

26

Whoa. Wow. I did it!

I really did it!

I really, really did it!

What a thrill! What a rush!

What a ride!

And I never even cried!

SPLOOSH!

The super slide was super fun!
And I couldn't have done it without
my COOL friends.

They all realized that I just needed
some encouragement and support.

Sometimes I forget that there are plenty
of kind folks who have my back.
They're always there
when I need them.
Yes, indeed.

And now it's time to relax

with my friends.

Because it turns out you

can be just as cool . . .

. . . at the shallow end of the pool.